irish
sayings

Designed by Tony and Penny Mills

irish
sayings

This edition published and distributed by Tara, 1999

Reprinted in 2000

Tara is an imprint of Parragon

Parragon
Queen Street House
4 Queen Street
Bath BA1 1HE

Produced by Magpie Books, an imprint of
Robinson Publishing Ltd, London

ISBN 1 90287 902 3

A copy of the British Library Cataloguing-in-Publication Data is available
from the British Library

Printed in China

ACKNOWLEDGEMENTS

Pictures on pp 9, 16, 18, 21, 22, 23, 31, 33, 35, 39, 43, 47, 48, 51 and
52 have been very kindly supplied by Celia Haddon.
We have been unable to trace the owners of certain copyrights and beg
the forgiveness of anyone whose rights have been overlooked.
We have been unable to trace the owners of certain copyrights and beg
forgiveness of anyone whose rights have been overlooked.

CONTENTS

Welcome   2

The Irish on Themselves   4

On Food & Eating . . .   8

. . . & Drinking   10

On Ageing   17

Animals   22

Women   28

Love & Marriage   30

Friends   38

Enemies   41

The Family   42

The Church   44

Work   46

Riches & Poverty   52

Ireland   54

introduction

The Irish have a tradition of wit and good humour
and it is no coincidence that they have produced
many of the most inventive and provocative writers
of the last century. Wilde, Shaw, Joyce and Beckett
came from a native culture that expressed in a quick
and pithy form a celebration of the things of good
value, hospitality, friendship and generosity, and an
amused intolerance of sham and humbug.

Many of the sayings gathered here have a uni-
versal truth and application, but the specific mixture
is quintessentially Irish: a deep respect for hospitality,
a delight in company and good fellowship, and an
almost mystic love of a country and people whose
traditions of deep religious belief and rich folklore
extend back into a legendary past.

welcome

We'll spread green rushes
under your feet.

Whoever comes to your door, you must
feed him or care for him,
with no questions asked.

OLD IRISH LAW

Won't you come into my garden?
I would like my roses to see you.

RICHARD BRINSLEY SHERIDAN

God, Mary and St Patrick greet
you and watch over you in our home.

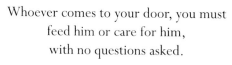

the irish on themselves

There are only two kinds of people
in the world,
The Irish,
And those who wish they were.

The reason the Irish are always
fighting each other
Is that they have no other
worthy opponents.

God invented whiskey
so the Irish wouldn't rule the world!

What is Irish diplomacy?
It's the ability to tell a man to go to Hell,
so that he will look forward
to making the trip.

If you're enough lucky to be Irish . . .
You're lucky enough!

A Tyrone woman will never buy a rabbit
without a head for fear it's a cat.

The Irish forgive their great men
when they are safely buried.

The Irish ne'er walk
But what they dance an Irish fling,
And Irish ne'er talk
But with lilting voices sing.

I am of Ireland,
And of the holy land
Of Ireland.
Good Sir, pray I thee,
For of saint charité
Come and dance with me,
In Ireland.

ANON (FOURTEENTH CENTURY)

on food & eating . . .

A trout in the pot is better than
a salmon in the sea.

The three most nourishing foods:
beef marrow, the meat of a chicken,
and Irish stout.

IRISH TRIAD

While we fatten and feast on
the smiling potatoes
of Erin's green valleys, so friendly to man.
Oh! there's not in the wide world
a race that can beat us,
From Canada's cold hills to sultry Japan.

REV JOHN GRAHAM

Only a foolish man would prefer
food to a woman.

Men are like bagpipes – no sound comes
from them until they're full.

. . . & drinking

He that buys land buys many stones.
He that buys flesh buys many bones.
He that buys eggs buys many shells.
But he that buys good beer
buys nothing else.

In Heaven there is no beer . . .
That's why we drink ours here.

Drunk is feeling sophisticated
when you can't say it.

Drink is the curse of the land.
It makes you fight with your neighbour.
It makes you shoot at your landlord
– and it makes you miss him.

What butter and whiskey will not cure,
there's no cure for.

A man that's fond of boozing,
His cash goes daily oozing;
His wife is unprotected,
His business is neglected,
So, do not get drunk any more.

It's nothing but folly
to treat an old woman
to a dram.

When two people tell you are drunk,
lie down.

Wine makes old women wenches.

Three things that are always ready in a
decent man's house:
beer, a bath, a good fire.

<small>IRISH TRIAD</small>

A narrow bottle neck
keeps the bottle from being emptied
in one swig.

O, long life to the man who
invented poteen,
Sure the Pope ought to make him a martyr.
If myself was this moment Victoria,
our Queen,
I'd drink nothing but whiskey and water.

MICHAEL MORAN

15

I have made an important discovery . . .
that alcohol, taken in sufficient quantities,
produces all the effects of intoxication.

OSCAR WILDE

ON AGEING

Do not mistake a goat's beard
for a fine stallion's tail.

The old pipe
gives the sweetest smoke.

A buckle is a great addition
to an old shoe.

No crocodile tears shall be shed
at my wake,
While there I am lying;
No counterfeit crying,
No moans, I desire, shall be made
for my sake.

The older the fiddle
the sweeter the tune.

It is better to die young than to outlive
all one loved, and all that rendered
one lovable.

COUNTESS OF BLESSINGTON

An old broom knows
the dirty corners best.

There never was an old slipper
but there was an old stocking
to match it.

AN OLD IRISH RECIPE FOR LONGEVITY

Leave the table hungry.
Leave the bed sleepy.
Leave the table thirsty.

Three things that are useless when old:
an old schoolmaster, an old horse,
and an old soldier.

IRISH TRIAD

When all your work is done,
May you sit down to your tea,
With your children's children
climbing on your knee.

animals

There was never a scabby sheep in a flock
that didn't like to have a comrade.

It's difficult to choose between
two blind goats.

It's a bad hen
that won't scratch herself.

As the old cock crows
the young cock learns.

Neither give cherries to pigs,
nor advice to a fool.

If I like a sow,
I like her litter.

No animal ever invented anything
as bad as drunkenness,
Or as good as drink!

If you lie down with dogs
you'll rise with fleas.

The fox never found a better messenger
than himself.

Better an ass that carries you
than a horse that throws you.

A town without a landlord or a bull
goes topsy-turvy.

Take a bull to a mansion
and it will go to the byre.

women

Disguise our bondage as we will,
'Tis woman, woman, rules us still.

THOMAS MOORE

It's as hard to see a woman crying as it is to
see a barefooted duck.

There'll be white blackbirds before an
unwilling woman ties the knot.

Women are stronger than men;
they do not die of wisdom.

They say women and music
should never be dated.

OLIVER GOLDSMITH

As a jewel in a pig's snout is a woman
without understanding.

O lovely Mary Donnelly, my joy, my
only best,

If fifty girls were 'round you,

I'd hardly see the rest.

WILLIAM ALLINGHAM

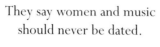

LOVE & MARRIAGE

My love is like a cabbage,
That's easy cut in two.
The leaves I'll give to others,
But the heart I'll keep for you.

ORAL POEM FROM TYRONE

Two children playing by a stream,
Two lovers walking in a dream,
A married pair who's dream is o'er,
Two old folks who are quite a bore.

ANNA PARNELL
Loves Four Ages

Money is the sinews of love,
as of war.

GEORGE FARQUHAR

Have you ever been in love, me boys,
O, have you felt the pain.
I'd rather be in jail, I would,
than be in love again.

JOHNNY PATTERSON
The Garden where the Praities Grow

It's a lonesome washing
without a man's shirt on it.

Three sparks that light the fire of love
are these:
Glamour of face, and grace,
and speech of ease.

IRISH TRIAD

There's no feast until a roast and no
torment until a marriage.

There's only one thing on earth better than
a good wife,
and that's no wife.

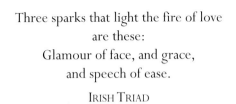

Better a wise wife
than a plough and land.

The blanket is the warmer
for being doubled.

Marriages are all happy.
It's having breakfast together
that causes all the trouble.

There's nothing in the world like the
devotion of a married woman. It's a thing
no married man knows anything about.

OSCAR WILDE

fRIENDS

Forsake not an old friend,
For the new is not comparable to him.
A new friend is as new wine –
When it is old, thou shalt drink it
with pleasure.

'Tis better to buy a small bouquet
And give to your friend this very day,
Than a bushel of roses white and red
To lay on his coffin after he's dead.

Friends should quarrel to strengthen
their attachment, and offend each other
for the pleasure of being reconciled.

MARIA EDGEWORTH

Always remember to forget
The things that made you sad,
But never forget to remember
The things that made you glad.
Always remember to forget
The friends that proved untrue,
But never forget to remember
Those that have stuck by you.
Always remember to forget
The troubles that passed away,
But never forget to remember.
The blessings that come each day.

Anybody can sympathise with the
sufferings of a friend, but it requires
a very fine nature to sympathise
with a friend's success.

OSCAR WILDE

enemies

Lord confound this surly sister,
Blight her brow with blotch and blister,
Cramp her larynx, lung and liver,
In her guts a galling give her.

JOHN MILLINGTON SYNGE

May your fire want for peat
and your children for meat.

Three men the devil can take without
much trouble – the mason, the bailiff
and the miller.

the family

Mothers hold their children's hands
for just a little while . . .
and their hearts forever.

A light-heeled mother makes
a leaden-heeled daughter.

There's no love until there's a family.

Many an Irish property was increased
by the lace of a daughter's petticoat.

the church

But if at church they give some ale,
And a pleasant fire for our souls to regale,
We'd sing and we'd pray all the live long day,
Nor ever once from the church to stray.

Be neither intimate nor distant
with the clergy.

Your priests, whate'er their
gentle shamming,
Have always had a taste for damning.

THOMAS MOORE

A dumb priest never got a parish.

If there's a hen or a goose,
It's surely on the priest's table
it will be.

WORK

MURPHY'S LAW

Nothing is as easy as it looks.
Everything takes longer than you expect.
And if anything can go wrong,
It will at the worst possible moment.

Work is the curse
of the drinking class.

OSCAR WILDE

If the knitter is weary,
The baby will have no new bonnet.

The early riser gets through his business,
But not through early rising.

An Irish Method for Tackling Problems

There comes a time
when you must take the bull
by the tail and face the situation squarely.

You must crack the nuts
before you can eat the kernel.

A windy day is not the day
for thatching.

There's no need to fear the wind
if your haystacks are tied down.

It's no use boiling your cabbage twice.

You'll never plough a field
by turning it over in your mind.

He who sows on a cold day
will not reap on a warm day.

riches & poverty

The rich man in his castle,
The poor man at his gate,
God made them high or lowly,
And ordered their estate.

CECELIA FRANCES ALEXANDER

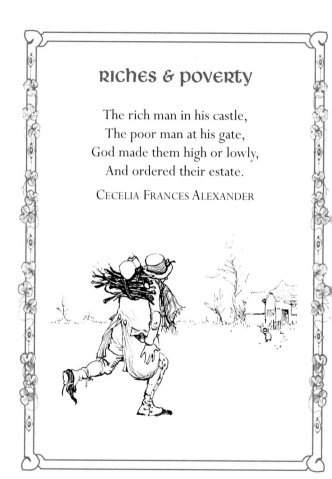

I complained that I had no shoes,
Until I met a man who had no feet.

It's no use carrying an umbrella
if your shoes are leaking.

Sweet is the voice
of the man who has wealth.

IRELAND

It may be some day I'll go back to Ireland,
If it's only at the closing of my day,
Just to see the moon rise over Claddagh,
And to watch the sun go down on
Galway Bay.

POPULAR SONG

This island is a region of
dreams and trifles.

GEORGE BERKELEY

Erin, the tear and the smile in thine eyes,
Blend like the rainbow that hangs
in the skies:
Shining through sorrows' stream,
Sadd'ning through pleasure's beam,
Thy suns with doubtful gleam,
Weep while they rise.

THOMAS MOORE

And still the thoughts of Ireland brood,
Upon her holy quietude.

JAMES CLARENCE MANGAN

Were all the tribute of Scotia mine,
From its midland to its borders,
I would give all for one little cell,
In my beautiful Derry.

ST COLUMCILL

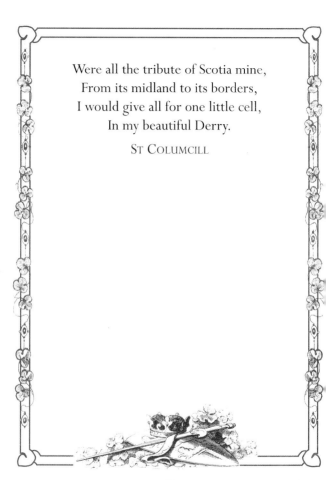